THE
PASSION
LIFE

BIBLE STUDY SERIES

THE
Psalms
1–41
POETRY ON FIRE

Book 1

12-WEEK STUDY GUIDE

BroadStreet
PUBLISHING

BroadStreet Publishing Group, LLC
Racine, Wisconsin, USA
BroadStreetPublishing.com

Passionate Life Bible Study
The Psalms 1–41: POETRY ON FIRE
BOOK 1 12-WEEK STUDY GUIDE

Copyright © 2016 BroadStreet Publishing Group

Edited by Jeremy Bouma

ISBN-13: 978-1-4245-5339-6 (softcover)
ISBN-13: 978-1-4245-5340-2 (e-book)

Cover design by Garborg Design at GarborgDesign.com
Typesetting by Katherine Lloyd at theDESKonline.com

Printed in the United States of America
16 17 18 19 20 5 4 3 2 1

Contents

Using This Passionate Life Bible Study 5

Introduction to the Genesis Psalms—Book I 9

Lesson 1   The Pathways of God's Pleasure vs. Man's Pleasure:
            Psalms 1, 2, 5 11

Lesson 2   Our True Hero, Champion Defender, and Healer:
            Psalms 3, 4, 6, and 7 18

Lesson 3   The Always-Hearing, Ready-to-Act God of the Oppressed:
            Psalms 8, 9, 11, and 12 25

Lesson 4   How Much Longer, Lord?: Psalms 10, 13, 17, and 20 32

Lesson 5   My Prize, My Pleasure, My Portion: Psalms 14, 15, and 16 39

Lesson 6   What Captures Your Heart?: Psalms 18, 19, and 21 45

Lesson 7   Don't Fear—Pray!: Psalms 22, 23, and 24 52

Lesson 8   Lord, Direct My Life-Path: Psalms 25, 26, and 27 59

Lesson 9   Into Your Hands I Entrust My Spirit:
            Psalms 28, 29, 30, and 31 67

Lesson 10   Celebrate the Goodness of God!:
            Psalms 32, 33, and 34 74

Lesson 11   Wait for the Lord, Then Wait Some More!:
            Psalms 35, 38, and 40 82

Lesson 12   Our Only Hope Is in the Lord!: Psalms 36, 37, 39, and 41 89

Using This Passionate Life Bible Study

The psalmist declares, "Truth's shining light guides me in my choices and decisions; the revelation of your Word makes my pathway clear" (Psalm 119:105).

This verse forms the foundation of the Passionate Life Bible Study series. Not only do we want to kindle within you a deep, burning passion for God and his Word, but we also want to let the Word's light blaze a bright path before you to help you make truth-filled choices and decisions, while encountering the heart of God along the way.

God longs to have his Word expressed in a way that would unlock the passion of his heart. Inspired by The Passion Translation but usable with any other Bible translation, this is a heart-level Bible study, from the passion of God's heart to the passion of your heart. Our goal is to trigger inside you an overwhelming response to the truth of the Bible, unfiltered by religious jargon.

DISCOVER. EXPLORE. EXPERIENCE. SHARE.

Each of the following lessons is divided into four sections: *Discover the Heart of God*; *Explore the Heart of God*; *Experience the Heart of God*; and *Share the Heart of God*. They are meant to guide your study of the truth of God's Word, while drawing you closer and deeper into his passionate heart for you and your world.

The *Discover* section is designed to help you make observations about the reading. Every lesson opens with the same three questions: What did you notice, perhaps for the first time? What questions do you have? And, what did you learn about the heart of God? There are no right answers here! They are meant to jump-start your journey into God's truth by bringing to

5

the surface your initial impressions about the passage. The other questions help draw your attention to specific points the author wrote and discover the truths God is conveying.

Explore takes you deeper into God's Word by inviting you to think more critically and explain what the passage is saying. Often there is some extra information to highlight and clarify certain aspects of the passage, while inviting you to make connections. Don't worry if the answers aren't immediately apparent. Sometimes you may need to dig a little deeper or take a little more time to think. You'll be grateful you did, because you will have tapped into God's revelation-light in greater measure!

Experience is meant to help you do just that: experience God's heart for you personally. It will help you live out God's Word by applying it to your unique life situation. Each question in this section is designed to bring the Bible into your world in fresh, exciting, and relevant ways. At the end of this section, you will have a better idea of how to make choices and decisions that please God, while walking through life on clear paths bathed in the light of his revelation!

The final section is *Share*. God's Word isn't meant to be merely studied or memorized; it's meant to be shared with other people—both through living and telling. This section helps you understand how the reading relates to growing closer to others, to enriching your fellowship and relationship with your world. It also helps you listen to the stories of those around you, so you can bridge Jesus' story with their stories.

SUGGESTIONS FOR INDIVIDUAL STUDY

Reading and studying the Bible is an exciting journey! Yet it isn't like studying for that American history, calculus, or chemistry class back in the day, where the goal was just fact gathering and memorizing information. Instead, think of this journey more like reading your favorite novel—where the purpose is encountering the heart and mind of the author through its characters and conflict, plot points, and prose.

This study is designed to help you encounter the heart of God and let his Word to you reach deep down into your very soul—all so you can live and enjoy the life he intends for you. And like with any journey, a number of practices will help you along the way:

1. Begin your lesson time in prayer, asking God to open up his Word to you in new ways, expose areas of your heart that need teaching and healing, and correct any area in which you're living contrary to his desires for your life.

2. Read the opening section to gain an understanding of the major themes of the reading and ideas for each lesson.

3. Read through the Scripture passage once, underlining or noting in your Bible anything that stands out to you. Reread the passage again, keeping in mind these three questions: What did you notice, perhaps for the first time? What questions do you have? What did you learn about the heart of God?

4. Write your answers to the questions in this Bible study guide or another place of choice. Take your time and don't get discouraged if you're unsure of an answer. If you do get stuck, first ask God to reveal his Word to you and guide you in his truth. And then, either wait until your small group time or ask your pastor or another teacher for help.

5. Use the end of the lesson to focus your time of prayer, thanking and praising God for the truth of his Word, for what he has revealed to you, and for how he has impacted your daily life.

SUGGESTIONS FOR SMALL GROUP STUDY

Think of your small group more like a book club rather than a group studying for a college class. The point isn't to memorize a list of facts and score points for right answers. The goal is to understand God's Word for you and your community in greater measure, while encountering his heart along the way. A number of practices will also help your group as you journey together:

1. Group studies usually go better when everyone is prepared to participate. The best way to prepare is to come having read the lesson's Scripture reading beforehand. Following the suggestions in each individual study will enrich your time as a community as well.

2. Before you begin the study, your group should nominate a leader to guide the discussion. While this person should work through the questions beforehand, his or her main job isn't to lecture, but to help move the conversation along by asking the lesson questions and facilitating the discussion.

3. This study is meant to be a community affair where everyone shares. Be sure to listen well, contribute where you feel led, and try not to dominate the conversation.

4. The number one rule for community interaction is: nothing is off-limits! No question is too dumb; no answer is out of bounds. While many questions in this study have "right" answers, most are designed to push you and your friends to explore the passage more deeply and understand what it means for daily living.

5. Finally, be ready for God to reveal himself through the passage being discussed and through the discussion that arises out of the group he's put together. Pray that he would reveal his heart and revelation-light to you all in deeper ways. And be open to being challenged, corrected, and changed.

Again, we pray and trust that this Bible study will kindle in you a burning, passionate desire for God and his heart, while impacting your life for years to come. May it open wide the storehouse of heaven's revelation-light. May it reveal new and greater insights into the mysteries of God and the kingdom-realm life he has for you. And may you encounter the heart of God in more fresh and relevant ways than you ever thought possible!

Introduction to the Genesis Psalms
Book 1

Every emotion of the heart is reflected in the Psalms with words that express our deepest and strongest feelings. They provide comfort and joy, leading us to the place where worship flows. *Poetry on Fire* is divided into five books, mirroring the Five Books of Moses that form the first few books of the Old Testament. Together they convey the depth of our longings and fears, joys and celebrations, becoming a mirror to the heart of God's people in our quest to experience God's presence.

Book One of Psalms is the Genesis Psalms, composed of poems and songs of man and creation. They explore the splendor of our world in all of its glory and grandeur, the way of righteousness versus the way of the wicked, and the glory and honor of mankind. You'll discover more of who our Creator is as our Best Friend, Good Shepherd, and Mighty One. There are songs of praise for God's goodness and glory. There are songs of lament for man's wickedness and injustice. And finally, there are prayers reflecting human frailty: the ones for help and healing, protection and provision, and trouble and thanksgiving.

We've designed this study to help you explore these praises and prayers placed inside poems that spill out of a fiery, passionate heart. May the study of this poetry on fire free you to become a passionate, sincere worshiper, and to experience the heart of God anew in faith and worship.

The Pathways of God's Pleasure vs. Man's Pleasure

PSALMS 1, 2, 5

What delight comes to those who follow God's ways!
They won't walk in step with the wicked, nor share the
sinner's way, nor sit in the circle of scoffers. ...
But how different are the wicked.
(Psalm 1:1, 4)

The opening lesson to Book One of Psalms could be considered an opening lesson to the book of Psalms itself, for these ancient poems comment on two opposing paths: the pathway of God's pleasures versus the pathway of man's.

One is reminded of something Jesus said: "Come to God through the narrow gate, because the wide gate and broad path is the way that leads to destruction—nearly everyone chooses that crowded road! The narrow gate and the difficult way leads to eternal life—so few even find it!" (Matthew 7:13–14).

Today we discover a similar contrast. Those who walk one path are like dust in the wind; nothing they do will succeed or endure. God merely laughs at their foolish plots, vowing to make an end of them. So the psalmist calls on these path walkers to serve and worship God. The other pathway, though, is much different. Those who walk it are blessed, for they hide themselves in God. These path walkers are like a flourishing, fruit-bearing tree planted by God's design.

Discover what the psalmist discovered: the pathways of men lead to destruction, but the pathways of God lead to his good pleasure.

Discover the Heart of God

- After reading Psalms 1, 2, and 5, what did you notice, perhaps for the first time? What questions do you have? What did you learn about the heart of God?

- What comes to those who follow God's ways rather than the ways of the wicked? What three words or actions are used in regard to following the ways of the wicked?

- Compare the difference between what happens in the life of the lovers of God versus the wicked.

- What do the nations plot and scheme against the Lord and his anointed? How does God respond?

- What is God's response to lawlessness and wicked people according to Psalm 5?

Explore the Heart of God

- Why do you think delight comes to the one who follows God's ways? Why is this person blessed? Why do the righteous stand firm "like a flourishing tree planted by God's design, deeply rooted by the brooks of bliss" (1:3)?

- How do you think it looks to walk, stand, and sit in the steps, ways, and company of the wicked? Why are the wicked like "dust in the wind"; why won't they "endure the day of judgment" (1:4, 5)?

- Many have understood Psalm 2:7–9 to refer to Christ. What does this prophetic psalm reveal about him?

- What does 2:10–12 reveal about the heart of God for rebel-kings and all rebellious people?

- Why does God hate what evildoers do; why does he "despise all who love violence" (5:6)?

- What does 5:8–12 reveal about what the righteous should pursue and expect from God? What about the wicked?

Experience the Heart of God

- Would you say you are more like the one who follows God's ways or the one who walks in step with the wicked? In what ways might you find yourself walking, standing, and sitting with sinners, rather than with God?

- Do you long to experience more of the heart of God found in Psalm 1:3—"never dry, never fainting, ever blessed, ever prosperous"? How would it look in your life to stand "firm like a flourishing tree" to experience the heart of God?

- In what ways do people plan and plot against the Lord Most High, like the rebel-kings? How have you?

- What lesson might the Lord want you to learn about serving, worshiping, and bowing before him?

- What comfort can you take from the heart of God to know that the righteous are covered by God's "canopy of kindness and joy" (5:12)?

Share the Heart of God

- Psalm 1 speaks of a delight that comes from following God's ways. Who do you know who needs to experience this delight in God's heart?

- Who in your life might you be tempted to follow who Psalm 1 would classify as wicked, a sinner, and a scoffer? How might it look to share with them the heart of God to guide their life to God's "brooks of bliss" (v. 3)?

- In what way do the fruit of our lives that are planted firmly like a flourishing tree help share the heart of God with those who are "dust in the wind" (v. 4)?

- How might the lives of rebels you know change if they heeded the words of Psalm 2:10-12, especially if you shared with them the blessing that awaits them?

- In Psalm 5, David gives two contrasting pictures of people: those who are guilty from collapse under rebellion and those who are glad from hiding themselves in the Lord. Pray for those you know who need to do the latter and escape the former.

CONSIDER THIS

There are two paths in life: one is the pathway of the righteous, the other is of the wicked. Robert Frost echoes the Hebrew poet: "Two roads diverged in a wood, and I—I took the one less traveled by, and that has made all the difference."[1] The road less traveled by does make all the difference, for it is the pathway of God's pleasures. Which path are you taking?

---

1   Robert Frost, "The Road Not Taken," in *Robert Frost: Collected Poems, Prose, and Plays* (New York: Library of America, 1995), 103.

Lesson 2

Our True Hero, Champion Defender, and Healer

PSALMS 3, 4, 6, AND 7

My true Hero comes to my rescue, for the Lord alone is my Savior.
What a feast of favor and bliss he gives his people!
(Psalm 3:8)

When you're in trouble, where do you turn for help? As a child, maybe you tried to call Batman or Superman to the rescue, but you probably relied on a parent or trusted adult to save you. As we get older we look to other "heroes" to rescue us: our friends, our employer, our culture, even our government.

Not David. David had many enemies who were against him, from Saul to his very own son Absalom. Yet from the depths of his heart he knew who was his true Shield: the Lord! He cried out to him from the depths of despair for help, and it was the Lord who came to his rescue as his true Hero. This is why every time he needed help, David ran to the Lord in prayer. He prayed that the Lord wouldn't condemn him or punish him in anger, but that he would heal him and restore him. He prayed that the Lord wouldn't leave him helpless and let his foes triumph over him, but that he would be his Champion Defender and Conqueror.

In this lesson, discover your true protection and defense; find your true Hero, Champion Defender, and Healer.

Discover the Heart of God

- After reading Psalms 3, 4, 6, and 7, what did you notice, perhaps for the first time? What questions do you have? What did you learn about the heart of God?

- According to Psalm 3, what did David truly know about God in the depths of his heart?

- What did David demand from God in Psalm 4?

- Why was David "so exhausted and worn-out" (6:6); why did sorrow fill his heart?

- Ultimately, why did David give his thanks to God in Psalm 7?

Explore the Heart of God

- Despite the many foes who rose up against David, why could he say "in the depths of my heart I truly know that you have become my Shield" (3:3)?

- In what way might bringing our gifts just as we are and putting our trust in the Lord be connected, as Psalm 4 suggests? What is the connection between worship and trust?

- What do you think David's question in Psalm 6:3 says about God's process in helping us? What does 6:8–9 say about this process?

- Why do you think David hid his soul in God, taking refuge in him and trusting him? What does this tell us about the heart of God?

- Read Psalm 7:10 again. What do you think this tells us about the heart of God?

Experience the Heart of God

- Have you experienced "many enemies" rising up against you, like David? If so, what was that like and how did you respond? Why don't we have to be afraid when dark powers and enemies prowl around us, and what do you think about David's prayer of help in Psalm 3:7?

- When you're in trouble, do you think of God as your "true Hero [who] comes to [your] rescue" (3:8) and your "Champion Defender" (4:1)? Why or why not?

- Have you ever wondered what David wondered: "Why aren't you answering me when I cry for help?" (4:1) or "How long ...?" (6:3)? Explain.

- How is it that you can be certain that God hears when you call and will answer every prayer?

- Can you relate to Psalm 6:6–7? How should 6:8–9 encourage and inform your experience of the heart of God?

- Do you actively view God as your "wrap-around presence" who is your "protection" and your "defense" (7:10)? If not, how might viewing God in this way deepen your experience of his heart?

Share the Heart of God

- Who do you know who seems to have so many enemies against them? How can you use Psalm 3 to encourage them?

- So many in our world don't have peace; they lead sleepless nights because of gripping fear. How might you encourage those you know with the heart of God in Psalm 4?

- Who do you know who is "so exhausted and worn-out with ... weeping" (6:6)? Now turn to the Lord on their behalf with a thunderous cry and ask the Lord to hear your pleadings for them.

- Consider someone you know who feels helpless and attacked. How is the heart of God revealed in 7:10 their best answer to their problems?

CONSIDER THIS

We don't need Superman or the State when we're in trouble. All we need is our true Champion Defender, our true Hero. The Lord Almighty! No matter what you may be going through, God is right beside you and will make everything right in the end. So spend time giving him your thanks and praise for what he will do—as much as for what he has already done!

Lesson 3

The Always-Hearing, Ready-to-Act God of the Oppressed

PSALMS 8, 9, 11, AND 12

All who are oppressed may come to you as a shelter
in the time of trouble, a perfect hiding place.
(Psalm 9:9)

We live in a day of oppression and exploitation. Whether economic or political, racial or ethnic, or even religious—oppression is a feature of our lives and the created order because of the wickedness of men and fallenness of creation.

Israel understood this well; their story was one of constant oppression. The book of Exodus opens with this very theme. God's people had grown numerous—so numerous that they threatened the established powers and economic balance. So the empire enslaved them, and they cried out to God for help. Exodus 2 says their cries drifted up to God like the smoke of a fragrant offering reaching every one of his senses. God saw their plight, heard their cries, and remembered his covenant with them. And then he acted.

You know what? He still does! This lesson blossoms with a bouquet of psalms testifying to the always-hearing, ready-to-act God who stands up for our cause, is a stronghold for the weak, saves the humiliated, and shelters the oppressed. We are invited to join David in not only offering our praise to the God of the oppressed but also offering our prayers to him. Just like Israel did.

Discover the Heart of God

- After reading Psalms 8, 9, 11, and 12, what did you notice, perhaps for the first time? What questions do you have? What did you learn about the heart of God?

- What did David wonder when he stared into the sky?

- What did David promise that all who are oppressed can find in God?

- What does 9:17–18 say we should never forget?

- What does the Lord closely watch while reigning from his temple of holiness?

- In Psalm 12, how did David describe every word God speaks?

Explore the Heart of God

- What does Psalm 8 teach us about how God uses creation to reveal himself? What does the psalm reveal about humanity, especially when it comes to how God views us?

- How is God's "dispensing justice to all" and his hearing cries of justice the reason why "all who are oppressed may come to [him] as a shelter in the time of trouble, a perfect hiding place" (9:8–9)?

- Why is what David's well-meaning friends said in 11:1-2 such a pessimistic view of life? How was David's response a good one?

- What does it tell us about the heart of God that, despite reigning from his holy temple in heaven, God still watches everything that happens on earth, as Psalm 11 says?

- What do you think David meant that "godly ones are swiftly disappearing. ... They're a vanishing breed!" (12:1)?

Experience the Heart of God

- When have you experienced the grandeur and glory of creation and just *known* that the God who made it all reigns over it?

- How does the description of humanity in Psalm 8 make you feel, especially to know you've been crowned with glory and magnificence?

- When you worship and praise God, do you do it like David, "with extended hands as [your] whole heart explodes with praise!" (9:1)? Do you "jump for joy and shout in triumph as [you] sing your song and make music for the Most High God" (v. 2)? How might Psalm 9 help guide how you worship?

- How does it make you feel to know God "will not ignore forever all the needs of the poor for those in need shall not always be crushed" (v. 18)? How does this shape your experience of the heart of God?

- Have you truly made God your only Hiding Place, as David had? If not, why, and how might you do so? If you have, how has doing so made all the difference to your experience of the heart of God?

- How might Psalm 12:6 be a sure and steady foundation to build your life upon, especially when all seems lost?

Share the Heart of God

- Part of the message of Psalm 8 is that every person on the planet is immensely important and valuable; we are known by God and crowned by God. How might sharing this with someone you know draw them closer to the heart of God?

- In what way can worship as pictured in 9:1–2, because of God's help and vindication, be a way you share the heart of God and help draw people into it?

- In what way might it be comforting for someone you know that God "is closely watching everything that happens" (11:4) in their own life?

- David reminds us that God defends the poor, the oppressed, and the needy. How might it look in your life to mirror this character of God to those who need defending, in order to share the heart of God with them?

CONSIDER THIS

Though this world can be oppressive, we can enter it each day knowing there is one who is far greater and more powerful: the always-hearing, ready-to-act God of the oppressed. He will shelter us and he will act to punish the oppressors. He will arise to help and rescue us because we are immensely valuable—just as he did for Israel and David.

Lesson 4

How Much Longer, Lord?

PSALMS 10, 13, 17, AND 20

I'm hurting, Lord—will you forget me forever?
How much longer, Lord? Will you look the other way when
I'm in need? How much longer must I cling to this constant grief?
(Psalm 13:1, 2)

How often do you long for God to do something about this broken world and the things that people do? We feel this burden when another terrorist bomb goes off—whether in our own country or someone else's. Or when a tsunami or hurricane decimates a coastal village. More often we feel it personally when evil encroaches on our lives through sickness, job loss, gossip, or death.

David sure felt this longing at different times in his life. He also wondered where on earth the Lord had gone. Perhaps you can relate. But you know what we discover in today's psalms? Something we can emulate in our own lives. With all the evil he witnessed and all the oppression he experienced, David asked the Lord, "How much longer?" He asked him why it seemed he stood so far off. He prayed that the Lord would punish the wicked. He cried out for justice. He told God he was hurting, and then asked him to do something about it.

We discover something else David did as well: he trusted. He believed that God would not only listen to him but also answer him. And that made all the difference.

Discover the Heart of God

- After reading Psalms 10, 13, 17, and 20, what did you notice, perhaps for the first time? What questions do you have? What did you learn about the heart of God?

- According to Psalm 10, what do the arrogant in their elitist pride do? What do they say in boast? What did the psalmist want the Lord to do in response?

- In Psalm 13, what did David ask in response to his need and grief? Why did David say he would eventually "celebrate with passion and joy" (13:5) and sing the Lord's praise?

- How did David describe his foes in Psalm 17? List the characteristics.

- At the start of Psalm 20, David prayed for seven things for God to do for him and his people. What were they?

Explore the Heart of God

- Why don't the orphans and the oppressed need to be terrified any longer? How will God help them? What does this say about the heart of God?

- Why do you suppose David cried out, "How much longer, Lord" (13:1)? What does this question reveal about his plight?

- In Psalm 17, what reason did David seem to have for coming to the Lord in prayer and asking him to help and hear him? Why was David so confident that he would be vindicated and see the Lord's face?

- Why do you think David invoked "the name of the God of Grace" or the "God of Jacob" (20:1) in regards to his protection? Why is that name a significant, protecting name?

- What does it mean for God to give us the desire of our heart, as Psalm 20:4 says?

- In what ways do people trust in their own "weapons and wisdom" (20:7) when life goes sour?

Experience the Heart of God

- Do you ever feel the Lord "seem[s] so far away when evil is near" (10:1)? That he stands so far off as if he doesn't care? Explain. In what way would you like the Lord to "arise" and crush the wicked, not forgetting the forgotten and helpless?

- Where in your life are you echoing David's cry, "How much longer?" Spend some time pouring your heart out to God, asking to experience his own heart in increasing measure.

- Do you trust that you will yet "celebrate with passion and joy" (13:5) when the Lord's salvation lifts you up? Explain.

- When you pray, do you use the same kind of "demanding" language that David did in Psalm 17? Why or why not?

- What heart desires do you long for God to give you? Write them down, then pray for them.

- In what chariots and horses, weapons and wisdom might you be trusting instead of in God alone? How might it look in your life to deliberately transfer your trust to the Lord your God?

Share the Heart of God

- Do you know anyone who is "poor and helpless" (10:2)? Why is Psalm 10:14, 17–18 such good news to those you know who are helpless and oppressed? How might it look to share the heart of God found in these verses?

- Who do you know who's asking, "How much longer, Lord?" Spend time praying for them, for their need and grief.

- Who do you know who needs God to arise and confront their foes? Spend time praying that the Lord would do that, that he would challenge those foes with his might, throw them down, and thrust them out of their prosperity.

- These psalms express absolute trust that God will deliver and bring victory. How might singing and proclaiming such trust be a way of sharing the heart of God with those you know?

CONSIDER THIS

Alongside David's cry for justice was a song of trust. Yes, he wondered where God was and when he would help. But he also declared, "I know God gives me all that I ask for and brings victory to his anointed king. My deliverance cry will be heard in his holy heaven" (20:6). May you feel the freedom to echo David's own cries while joining him in his declaration of trust.

Lesson 5

My Prize, My Pleasure, My Portion

PSALMS 14, 15, AND 16

Lord, I have chosen you alone as my inheritance.
You are my prize, my pleasure, and my portion.
I leave my destiny and its timing in your hands.
(Psalm 16:5)

Our lives are filled to the brim with trinkets that sing for our heart's attention, trying to fill the God-shaped hole in all of us. The typical, obvious dangers like money and possessions have been wrapping themselves around our souls like tentacles from the dawn of time. But there are less obvious newer ones too. Social networking sites, for instance, promise instant praise and adoration, feeding our longing to be liked and applauded.

These two examples illustrate something that today's lesson teaches: from the beginning of our creation, God has longed to be enough for us—which we try to deny at every turn. Some people insist there is no God and live as if that's true. Some imagine their "Safe Place" (16:1) is rooted in the above examples of money and social approval. Others presume the privilege of being close to God and finding what they need in him but don't want to do what the Lord requires of them.

Discover below what it means and how it looks to choose the Lord alone as our inheritance—to find in him our prize, our pleasure, and our portion.

Discover the Heart of God

- After reading Psalms 14, 15, and 16, what did you notice, perhaps for the first time? What questions do you have? What did you learn about the heart of God?

- What kind of person says, "There is no God"? What is this person who thinks like this?

- When God looks down on earth at the people below, what does he find?

- In Psalm 15, how did David describe the ones who are able to dwell with the Lord and be close to him?

- What did David ask God to do for him in Psalm 16? What did David say the Lord was for him in this psalm?

Explore the Heart of God

- What does it tell us about humanity that when God searches the world for "anyone who acts wisely, any who are searching for God and wanting to please him," he finds that "not one is good" and everyone has wandered astray (14:2, 3)?

- Why do you think David is right, that "the Lord is on the side of the generation of loyal lovers" (v. 5)?

- Why is it that the people David described in Psalm 15 "will never be shaken; they will stand firm forever" (v. 5)?

- What does it mean that God is our "Safe Place" (16:1), that in him we can take refuge?

- What do you think David meant when he said the Lord is "my prize, my pleasure, and my portion" (v. 5)?

Experience the Heart of God

- How have you seen evidence of the truth of Psalm 14:2–3? How might you experience the heart of God in the midst of this evil, especially in light of 14:6–7?

- In Psalm 15, David explains the ones who have the privilege of being close to the Lord. How do you compare?

- When you are in trouble, do you run to God as your first place of refuge? Is he your ultimate "Safe Place"? Why or why not? Explain.

- Do you echo David's declaration in Psalm 16:5 with your own life? How might it impact your experience of the heart of God if you did?

- What does it mean to you that God "will not abandon [you] to the realm of death nor will [he] allow [his] Holy One to experience corruption" (v. 9)?

Share the Heart of God

- Who do you know who says to themselves, "There is no God"? Why do you think they say this?

- Part of what David is saying in Psalm 14 is that despite human injustice, God's justice and rescue will come. How might it look to share this aspect of the heart of God with the world around you?

- Who do you know who is in need of the "Safe Place" the Lord provides? What can you share with them this week to share this aspect of the heart of God?

- Consider again someone you know who needs a Safe Place. How might your own confidence and joy in God's resurrection-life be a way to share God's heart with them?

CONSIDER THIS

David is right: there is no one who seeks God, not even one! Not only has humanity wandered astray, stubbornly walking in evil, but they also find their dwelling and satisfaction in everything but the Lord. May we join David in not only daily dwelling with the Lord; may we also find our inheritance in the Lord—making him our prize, pleasure, and portion forever!

Lesson 6

What Captures Your Heart?

PSALMS 18, 19, AND 21

So may the words of my mouth, my meditation-thoughts,
and every movement of my heart be always pure
and pleasing, acceptable before your eyes,
my only Redeemer, my Protector-God.
(Psalm 19:14)

This lesson picks up on a theme from the last one: what has captured our heart. For some people, *things* have captured them; they delight in the objects of the world, what material items can do for them and how they make them feel. For others who have rejected God, saying, "There is no God!" *they* have captured their heart; they delight in themselves and lean on themselves for help.

Not David. His heart was captured by the Lord, and David wanted more of God's heart to meditate upon him and his ways. One reason why was because of what God had done for him. He had reached down from heaven and showed up in very tangible ways, delivering and rescuing him. David was also captivated by what he saw of God in creation. And then there was God's Word, which he thought was like the rarest treasures of the finest gold; there was nothing sweeter to him than the revelation-truth found in it, and he savored it.

45

Find what David found in the Lord by exploring and discovering what the heart of God means for you and your life.

Discover the Heart of God

- After reading Psalm 18, 19, and 21, what did you notice, perhaps for the first time? What questions do you have? What did you learn about the heart of God?

- In Psalm 18:1–2, David listed a number characteristics of God to extol all the ways God had meant to him. List them here.

- What are all of the things God has done for us that are proof "there is not a more secure foundation to build [our] life upon than [the Lord]" (18:31)?

- According to Psalm 19, what story do the heavens declare, what tale "is written in the stars" (v. 1)? How did David describe God's Word in Psalm 19—what is it like, what does it do for us, and how had it captured David's heart?

- How did God respond to David's "heart's desire" in Psalm 21? How did the kings respond to God?

Explore the Heart of God

- Psalm 18 gives us some amazing imagery of God. How do these images amplify how God exercises his power on our behalf and his heart toward us?

- In what way is God's deliverance and our obedience connected in Psalm 18? How should this shape our lives before we are in distress?

- In Psalm 18 and 21, there is a lot of talk about defeating enemies, even "pulverizing them to powder!" (18:42). Does it surprise you that God would allow and entertain this? What does this reveal about the heart of God?

- David revealed that we are able to know God through creation, because his "truth is on tour in the starry-vault of the sky" (19:1). What can we learn about God through creation's message?

- In what way does God's Word "revive the soul," "lead us to truth," "change the simple to wise," and "make us joyful" (19:7)? How might this revelation-truth about God's Word capture our heart, informing the distress and deliverance we find in Psalm 18 and 21?

- What does it mean that God had given David his "heart's desire, anything and everything he asks for" (21:2)? Does God always do this? Explain. What does this reveal about the heart of God?

Experience the Heart of God

- In Psalm 18:1–2, which of David's descriptions do you resonate with the most? Are there any you don't fully trust are true about God? Why not? Which do you want God to be the most for you at this point in your life?

- When was the last time you cried out to the Lord in your distress and darkness, and experienced God's deliverance and rescue? What was that like?

- What do you think about the idea that "how we live will dictate how [the Lord deals] with us" (18:25)? How should this shape your experience of the heart of God?

- Do you view God's Word as David did, as the "rarest treasure of life," "the finest gold," and "sweetness" (19:10)? Has it captured your heart? Why or why not?

- Read Psalm 21:7 again. Do you join the king in trusting endlessly in the Lord? Do you believe deep down that God's forever-love never fails?

Share the Heart of God

- Who do you know who needs to know that all they need to do is call to the Lord, and when they do they'll be safe and sound in him? Commit this week to sharing this revelation-truth with them.

- In many ways, Psalm 18 is an example of a testimony, an authentic sharing of God's power and presence in our lives. While every Christian has multiple testimonies, what is one you can convey to someone to share the heart of God, just like David did with us?

- Sometimes it can be difficult to find common ground and a good starting place with unbelievers when it comes to sharing the heart of God. How might the opening verses in Psalm 19 be ground you can use to start a conversation about God and his love?

- David reveals in our reading that God's Word revives, leads, teaches, challenges, and helps us shine. What are some passages you feel are perfect for sharing the heart of God? List them here and commit to memorizing a few.

- Psalm 21 reminds us that those we know can trust endlessly in the Lord, for they will never stumble because of Gods forever-love. Pray that the person in the first question in this section would experience this same trust.

CONSIDER THIS

Consider David's question and answer: "Could there be any other god like you? You are the only God to be worshiped, for there is not a more secure foundation to build my life upon than you" (18:31). The truth is, we build our life upon whatever captures our heart. So how are you building? What has captured your heart?

Lesson 7

Don't Fear—Pray!

PSALMS 22, 23, AND 24

The Lord is my Best Friend and my Shepherd.
I always have more than enough. He offers a resting place
for me in his luxurious love. His tracks take me to
an oasis of peace, the quiet brook of bliss.
(Psalm 23:1–2)

In 1855, Joseph M. Scriven wrote his mother a poem to comfort her during a time of illness. She was living in Ireland while he was living in Canada. He had left his home to start another life across the ocean after his fiancée died the day before their wedding. Here is what he wrote:

What a Friend we have in Jesus, all our sins and griefs to bear!
What a privilege to carry everything to God in prayer!
O what peace we often forfeit, O what needless pain we bear,
All because we do not carry everything to God in prayer.[1]

This poem, forged in the fires of personal suffering, would become the song "What a Friend We Have in Jesus," a hymn that's comforted countless people. It reflects what David himself had learned through suffering and taking countless causes to God in prayer. When he was hunted by enemies,

---

1   Joseph M. Scriven, "What a Friend We Have in Jesus," 1855, audio recording, public domain.

he prayed; when he was downcast and feeling hopeless, he prayed; when darkness was close and death even closer, he prayed.

And what did he learn through it all? We don't have to fear when we turn to our Best Friend, our Good Shepherd.

Discover the Heart of God

- After reading Psalm 22, 23, and 24, what did you notice, perhaps for the first time? What questions do you have? What did you learn about the heart of God?

- In Psalm 22, what did David realize was true about his entire life, from infancy to adulthood?

- In this psalm, David is clearly in the depths of despair; he is like a crushed, bleeding worm. List all the ways he described his agonizing experience throughout this cry for help.

- In what ways is God described as our Best Friend and our Shepherd in Psalm 23? List them here.

- Why is it that we don't have to fear "the valley of deepest darkness," as Psalm 23 says?

- God is not only our Good Shepherd but also our Glorious King! How did David describe him in this way in Psalm 24?

Explore the Heart of God

- David obviously felt abandoned in Psalm 22. Yet he knew two things: God was most holy and enthroned, and Israel's ancestors put their faith in him. How might these two truths have informed David's experience of the heart of God?

- What does it tell us about the heart of God that the Lord "delivered me safely from my mother's womb" and "cared for me ever since I was a baby" (22:9)? How should this inform our experience of his heart when our courage has vanished and we need rescue?

- Psalm 22 is a famous psalm because Jesus quoted it from the cross. How is it a breathtaking portrayal of what Jesus endured through his suffering and crucifixion?

- The word most commonly used in Psalm 23:1 for shepherd is *ra'ah,* which is also the Hebrew word for "best friend." What does it say about the heart of God that he is described as our Best Friend, our Shepherd?

- As our Glorious King, how should we receive the Lord? How does the figure of speech of lifting and opening gates explain this reception?

Experience the Heart of God

- When have you resonated with David's questions in Psalm 22:1: "Why would you abandon me?", "Why do you remain distant?", and "Where are you, my God?" Explain.

- Sometimes we need to look back at the faith that others before us had in the Lord. Who in your life can you look to in order to find strength for your own faith when life gets tough and you fear?

- Hebrews 12:2–3 encourages us to "fasten our gaze onto Jesus who birthed faith within us and who leads us forward into faith's perfection," mostly because "he endured the agony of the cross and conquered its humiliation." How might meditating on Christ's own experience of suffering, as alluded to in Psalm 22, help you experience the heart of God more deeply?

- Of the ways our Best Friend and Shepherd cares for us, which do you resonate with the most? Which do you *need* the most, right now? Now pray he would provide this for you.

- How might it look in your life to receive God as your Glorious King? What can you do practically to lift the gate of your heart and welcome the King of Glory?

Share the Heart of God

- God knows what it's like to feel and be abandoned, because he himself was abandoned. How might this truth encourage someone you know who is exhausted and spent?

- In Psalm 22, David declared that the Lord is our only might and strength. Where do people often run to find such strength in order to be rescued when life goes dark? What from Psalm 22 can you use to share with them the heart of God?

- Psalm 23 is one of the most popular and well-known psalms because it speaks to the depths of human pain and misery, offering hope and comfort. Spend time memorizing it so you can offer it to those you know who need the heart of God it offers.

- What in Psalm 23 can provide those you know with hope and a better understanding of the heart of God? Now share one nugget of revelation-truth with someone you know so they don't have to fear the future.

- Psalm 24 is clear that "those whose hearts are true and sealed by the truth" (24:4) can receive the Lord's blessing and enjoy his presence. How might it look for you to help others receive the King of Glory, perhaps for the first time?

CONSIDER THIS

In this lesson we are invited to not only pray to God but also praise him by flinging wide open the gates of our heart, for our Best Friend and Good Shepherd is ready and worthy to receive our worship. After all, not only is he our Friend and Shepherd, but he is also the Lord of Victory, the Mighty One, the King of Glory who drives our fear away!

Lesson 8

Lord, Direct My Life-Path

PSALMS 25, 26, AND 27

Lord, direct me throughout my journey so
I can experience your plans for my life. Reveal the life-paths
that are pleasing to you. Escort me along the way; take me by
the hand and teach me. For you are the God of my
increasing salvation; I have wrapped my heart into yours!
(Psalms 25:4–5)

In the ancient world, there were two lists that categorized separate ways of living: a vice list and a virtue list. Vices included cowardice and theft, gluttony and greed; virtues included courage and truth, modesty and responsibility.

Book One of the psalms echoes this ancient worldview. David wanted nothing more than Yahweh's help to walk the life-path that would take him straight into God's pleasure. He wanted God to escort him along this path, taking him by the hand and teaching him how to walk it. He recognized the Lord was his Revelation-Light who would guide him along the way, so he wanted more of him. While walking this path, David promised to deny the company of sinners—to despise where they hung out and refuse to enter their domain. And along the way he wanted the Lord to show him grace and mercy, forgiving the failures of his youth.

Explore how you can walk the proper life-path that leads to God's pleasure and virtue. Discover the way of safety and security.

Discover the Heart of God

- After reading Psalms 25, 26, and 27, what did you notice, perhaps for the first time? What questions do you have? What did you learn about the heart of God?

- In light of putting his trust in God, according to Psalm 25 what did David want in response?

- According to Psalm 26, how did David say he lived? What kind of life did he claim he lived?

• What did David confidently declare in Psalm 27?

• What was "the one thing" David craved from God in Psalm 27, "the one thing" he sought above all else?

• According to Psalm 27, what had David ultimately learned through all of his abandonment and trouble?

Explore the Heart of God

• Why isn't anyone disgraced who has "entwined their hearts" (25:3) with the Lord? In what way are those who hope in the Lord not put to shame?

- Why is it true of the Lord that "when someone turns to [him], they discover how easy [he is] to please—so faithful and true!" (25:8)? What does this say about the heart of God?

- Why do you think David asked the Lord to test and try him, to scrutinize and probe his heart and thoughts? What did he hope the Lord would find?

- What do you think it means and how does it look to lead a blameless life, choosing "to walk only in what is right" (26:11)? How did David connect such living with his request for the Lord to "save me, redeem me with your mercy" (26:11)?

- Why was David able to confidently declare, "I fear no one!" (27:1)?

- What does it look like to crave and seek "the one thing" David himself did in Psalm 27:4?

Experience the Heart of God

- David asked the Lord to forgive the sins and failures of his youth and immaturity. Can you relate? If so, what would you like him to forgive and overlook?

- In Psalm 25:8 David said, "When someone turns to you, they discover how easy you are to please—so faithful and true!" Jesus said something similar: "Learn my ways and you'll discover that I'm gentle, humble, easy to please. You will find refreshment and rest in me" (Matthew 11:29). What do you think about this aspect of the heart of God and his life-path? How have you yourself experienced it?

- What do you think about David's challenge to God to "scrutinize" him and "probe" his every thought? How do you think you'd stand up under such testing?

- David said he lived a blameless life, having "chosen to walk only in what is right" (26:11). Can you claim the same? Why or why not? How do you think walking such a life-path would impact your experience of the heart of God?

- Do you crave and seek the same thing David did in Psalm 27:4? Explain.

• What sort of thing are you waiting for, like David did? How might it look to not give up, as David encouraged in Psalm 27:14? How should this psalm draw you closer to the heart of God?

Share the Heart of God

• Who do you know who still struggles with the shame from their sins and failures? How might sharing Psalm 25 with them draw them closer to the heart of God?

• Do you think that most people outside the church believe Psalm 25:6 to be true? Why or why not? How can you show them that it is, in order to show them the heart of God?

- David said he would proclaim publicly that he had "chosen to walk only in what is right" (26:11). Why might following his example be important to sharing the heart of God? How might it look for you to do so?

- Go back to your answer from the fourth question in the previous section. How might craving the things of God be crucial to sharing the heart of God? How can you invite others to join you in such craving?

- Who do you know who is like an orphan, abandoned by their father and mother as David was? How can you share with them the heart of God, who takes people in and makes them his?

CONSIDER THIS

David unveils a secret in this lesson: "There's a private place reserved for the lovers of God where they sit near him and receive the revelation-secrets of his promises" (Psalm 25:14). Crave that place, and seek that place in order to walk the Lord's life-path of peace and prosperity. Ask the Lord for guidance and direction along the way.

Lesson 9

Into Your Hands
I Entrust My Spirit

PSALMS 28, 29, 30, AND 31

For you are my high Fortress where I'm kept safe.
You are to me a stronghold of salvation. When you deliver me
out of this peril, it will bring glory to your name. ...
Into your hands I now entrust my spirit. O Lord, the God
of faithfulness, you have rescued and redeemed me.
(Psalm 31:3–5)

There is an undeniable quality about our created world and human condition: tragedy will strike. Someone close to you may die too early. Your company may downsize and you'll have to find another job. Someone close to you may hurt you with their words or actions. The doctor may call with test results that sends your family into a panic.

When tragedy strikes, into whose hands do you entrust yourself? It seems this is a question that David himself asked seemingly constantly. He was faced with one tragic situation after another—sometimes caused by his own hand but often the result of vicious enemies. Yet through it all David made a conscious choice: "Into your hands I now entrust my spirit." Why? Because through the course of David's life, the Lord, the God of faithfulness, had rescued and redeemed him. Yes, he pleaded with the Lord for help, but he also trusted him for it. The reason he did is because the Glory-God reigns.

Today's lesson offers us two kinds of psalms that direct our attention to this conscious committing, as well as the reason for that choice: the goodness and greatness of God.

Discover the Heart of God

- After reading Psalm 28, 29, 30, and 31, what did you notice, perhaps for the first time? What questions do you have? What did you learn about the heart of God?

- What are all the ways that David identified God in Psalm 28? List them here.

- Why did David exalt the Lord in Psalm 30? Why did David tell the steadfast lovers of God to give God thanks and sing his praises?

- What happened when David boasted, "I've got it made!" (30:6)?

- In Psalm 31, why did David throw himself upon God in trust?

Explore the Heart of God

- What do you think it means that God was David's Rock and Defender, that he was the Inner Strength and Fortress of Salvation for his people? What does this reveal about the heart of God?

- Why do you think David wanted God to repay the wicked with evil in proportion to their wickedness? What do you think about this? Is this an appropriate thing to pray for?

- What do you think the voice of God represents in Psalm 29? What does it evoke, and how does it reveal the heart of God?

- Why should all believers join David in exalting the Lord and singing and making melody to him?

- Despite David's boasting in his security, there was a point when God hid his face from him. Why, and how did David respond? How does the Lord's own response reveal his heart to us?

- What is the dominant theme of Psalm 31? How might verse 15 connect to that theme?

Experience the Heart of God

- When was the last time you pleaded with God for help and asked him to "please listen to my cry" (28:2)? How did you experience the heart of God in his answer?

- How have you personally witnessed and experienced the names David called the Lord in Psalm 28: Shield and Inner Strength, Mighty Provider and Saving Strength?

- How does your worship of God in response to his power and voice compare to the call David made in Psalm 29 and 30?

- Was there ever a time when you thought you had it made—thinking like David, "Nothing can stop me now!"—but then you fell from a place of safety? How did the Lord still show his mercy toward you by sharing his heart with you?

- How do you think it would look for you to "Cheer up! Take courage. ... Wait for the Lord to break through for you" (31:24)?

Share the Heart of God

- Do you know anyone who is pleading with the Lord for help? How can Psalm 28 help them experience the heart of God?

- Sometimes we need to join with other sons and daughters of Almighty God and proclaim his majesty! Who can you get together with to "be in awe before his majesty" and "give him the honor due his name" (29:2) together?

- Someone you know needs to experience the heart of God through your praise of God. With whom can you share the evidence of God's "famous mercy" (30:10), explaining why you can never thank him enough?

- Psalm 31 is a psalm of trust because of the Lord's faithfulness in the midst of exhaustion and sorrow. How might it look to help someone you know trust God enough to throw themselves upon him, knowing their destiny is in his hands?

CONSIDER THIS

David provides a profound example of how it looks and what it means to consciously entrust ourselves to the Lord, especially when tragedy strikes. Alongside David is another: Jesus. He uttered the same words from Psalm 31 while hanging on the cross; he entrusted his spirit to God the Father. If the Son of God recognized that this moment, and his destiny, was in God's hands, then why can't we?

Lesson 10

Celebrate the Goodness of God!

PSALMS 32, 33, AND 34

So celebrate the goodness of God!
He shows this kindness to everyone who is his! Go ahead—
shout for joy, all you upright ones who want to please him!
(Psalm 32:11)

One of the things that the psalms helps us with is not only giving voice to our prayers but also to our praise. They teach us to get our praise on as much as our praying on! And today's poems teach us both the *how* and the *why* of praise.

First, the how. David encourages us to not only sing for joy but also to shout our joyous praises. We should praise God with all we have, which includes our voices and our instruments. Break out the guitar and the drums, use the organ and the piano, toot on trumpets and trombones. With whatever instruments we have and however we've been skilled, we should make the Lord famous and make his name glorious!

And now the why. Why should we take so much time to expend such energy and skill? Yes, because of who he is as Yahweh, our awe-inspiring

Creator. But also because of what he's done—for us! He's blessed and prospered us, strengthened and delivered us. Most of all, he's forgiven our rebellion, covered our sins with Christ's blood, and wiped our slate clean.

If that's not a reason to sing and shout, what is?

Discover the Heart of God

- After reading Psalm 32, 33, and 34, what did you notice, perhaps for the first time? What questions do you have? What did you learn about the heart of God?

- Who are those who are happy and fulfilled, blessed and relieved?

- What has God done with the sins and rebellious acts of those who have confessed them? What happened when David finally admitted to God all his sins? What did he learn from it?

- What are the ways David called upon "all you redeemed ones" to "sing and shout for joy" (33:1)?

- According to Psalm 34, how did David respond to what the Lord did for him? According to his test, what did he do for David?

- What did David promise those who fear the Lord? What about those who don't?

Explore the Heart of God

- Why is it that people "whose rebellion has been forgiven" and "whose sins are covered by blood" (32:1) are happy and fulfilled, blessed and relieved?

- What does unconfessed sin do to us? Why do you think that is? How do we escape this?

- In what way did David connect singing and shouting for joy to redemption in Psalm 33?

- How is it we can "live a long, good life, enjoying the beauty that fills each day" (34:12–13)? How does this look in the day-to-day, and how does it ensure that good life?

- Why do you suppose the Lord opposes evildoers? What does this reveal about the heart of God?

Experience the Heart of God

- When was a time you needed the forgiveness of God for your sins? How did you feel before confessing them to God? What about afterward?

- How does it deepen your experience of the heart of God to know that when we admit to the Lord all our sins, "all at once the guilt of [our] sin washe[s] away and all [our] pain disappeare[s]" (32:5)?

- David insisted that God's redemption and his Word are "something to sing about" (33:4). Does your own worship reflect this reality?

- David tells everyone to worship Yahweh, but worship can be different for different people. How do you like to worship God? How can you give God more of that worship this week?

- In Psalm 34, David invites us to "listen to my testimony" (34:4) about the Lord hearing him in his distress. What would you want others to listen to regarding a similar time of deliverance in your own life?

Share the Heart of God

- Talking about sin isn't the most comfortable thing to do, but how might sharing the revelation-truth in Psalm 32 actually be a way of sharing the heart of God?

- Do you know anyone whose life is "filled with frustration, irrepressible anguish, and misery" (32:3) because they are keeping unconfessed sin inside? How might sharing an experience you've had with confession open an opportunity to share with them the heart of God?

- David said, "Let everyone worship Yahweh" (33:8) for who he is and what he's done. This week, who in your life can you invite to praise the Lord with all they have?

- How can a testimony about when you sought the Lord and he listened to your distress be the perfect opportunity to share the heart of God with those you know?

• Why might it be important for those you know that the Lord "watches over his friends day and night," but he "has made up his mind to oppose evildoers" (34:15–16)?

CONSIDER THIS

Go ahead, "compose new melodies that release new praises to the Lord!" (Psalm 33:3). Let us burst and boast with all that we are because of who God is and what God has done, for "the Lord has paid for the freedom of his servants, and he will freely pardon those who love him. He will declare them free and innocent when they turn to hide themselves in him" (34:22).

Lesson 11

Wait for the Lord, Then Wait Some More!

PSALMS 35, 38, AND 40

I waited and waited and waited some more; patiently,
knowing God would come through for me.
Then, at last, he bent down and listened to my cry.
(Psalm 40:1)

They say good things come to those who wait. After thirty-nine weeks, a mom and dad have a new bundle of joy. After a four-year-long college program, there's usually a good job in store. Yet in our increasingly on-demand, instant-gratification world, patience is no longer a virtue. David aims to remedy this.

This lesson opens in a similar way to most of the previous ones: David was in trouble. This time he was being harassed and accused, and he wanted the Lord to fight for him, to put on his armor and rise up against his enemies. Then in Psalm 38 David was sick with fever, his strength sapped. But in the final psalm his tune changed: God came through for him! David sang the praises of the One who not only heard him but also delivered him. All because he waited and waited, then waited some more.

David recognized the only thing he could do in the midst of trouble was to wait for the Lord's help and put his hope in him. When he did, he received what we all do—the blessings of the Lord poured out from the storehouses of heaven!

Discover the Heart of God

- After reading Psalms 35, 38, and 40, what did you notice, perhaps for the first time? What questions do you have? What did you learn about the heart of God?

- In Psalm 35, what did David want the Lord to do for him in response to those who had "devised their plans to disgrace" him (v. 4)? List all the ways here.

- In Psalm 38, how did David describe the Lord's rebuke, wrath, and discipline brought on by his sin?

- What did David do in response to the Lord's conviction and rebuke? What did he ask for the Lord to do?

- What happened after David patiently "waited and waited and waited some more" (40:1)? How did David describe those "who love and trust the Lord" (v. 4)?

Explore the Heart of God

- How do you think the Lord fulfills the requests we find in Psalm 35? How does he fight for us?

- What does it tell you about the heart of God that he protects "the weak and helpless from the strong and heartless who oppress them" (35:10)?

- Based on 35:16 and 22, what does God sometimes do in the midst of our trouble? What is still true of God even though he acts in this way?

- Why did David experience what he did at the hand of the Lord because of his sin? Why do we?

- Why is it that burnt offerings and sin offerings don't really move the Lord's heart or bring him joy? What does instead?

Experience the Heart of God

- When have you echoed David's request, "Lord, fight for me! Now is the time to act!" (35:1, 17)? What was that like? When did he come and rescue you, and what was that like?

- How should it impact your experience of the heart of God to know that the Lord protects "the weak and helpless from the strong and heartless who oppress them" (35:10)?

- Psalm 35 is the first of seven psalms in which David cried out for vengeance upon his enemies. Do you have enemies of your own? Spend time praying for them, as Jesus said in Matthew 5. Then trust the Lord to rise up and vindicate you.

- When was a time you were "overwhelmed, swamped, and submerged beneath the heavy burden" of guilt and God's conviction over sin (38:4)? What was that like? How did you experience the heart of God in the midst of it?

- Have you ever felt as if "evil surrounds [you]; problems greater than [you] can solve come one after another" (40:12)? What do you do when you feel this way? How might calling on the Lord to come quickly and rescue you solve what you yourself can't and help you experience his heart in increasing measure?

Share the Heart of God

- Who do you know who needs someone to fight for them, to do something and act on their behalf? Pray that God would come to their rescue, but also share with them the heart of God found in Psalm 35.

- Reconsider the previous question. How might it look to act as the Lord's presence in their life by not only sharing the heart of God but also showing it too? How can you fight for them as an ambassador of Christ?

- Who do you know who is overwhelmed by suffering under guilt or completely broken because of sin? How might you share with them the heart of God and revelation-truth found in Psalm 38?

- In Psalm 40:21–22, David asked the Lord not to forsake him but to "hurry to help me, run to my rescue!" In the context of this passage on sin and guilt, God did this through Jesus! How might it look to share the hope of this Help and Rescue with the person you know in the previous question?

- Waiting for help and rescue is never pleasant, but Psalm 40 reminds us we should, and to trust God in the process. This week, how can you encourage someone you know in their waiting for God to help lift them out of danger?

CONSIDER THIS

How are you at waiting, whether for relief from suffering or release from sin? Do you have the perspective of David, that "the only thing I can do is wait and put my hope in you. I wait for your help, my God" (38:15)? Or do you take matters into your own hands? May we remember that blessings come to those who love and trust the Lord!

Lesson 12

Our Only Hope Is in the Lord!

PSALMS 36, 37, 39, AND 41

And now, God, I'm left with one conclusion.
My only hope is to hope in you alone!
(Psalm 39:7)

Hope is hard to come by these days. From constant unemployment to underemployment, hope clearly isn't found in our economy. Government job approval ratings across the world prove that people don't hope much in politics either. Technology was supposed to solve our problems, yet we're busier and more stressed than ever!

We end our exploration of Book One of the psalms with an important question: where do you put your hope? King David draws our attention to a number of things that are hope-less, urging us not to misplace hope in these empty promises. Bringing us back to the beginning, he reminds us that hope isn't in the pathway of the wicked, for they are "crooked and conceited" (36:2). It isn't found in wealth either, for that shrivels and fades away. We shouldn't even hope in ourselves, for our lives are limited and fleeting.

After exploring this lesson, you will be left with the only conclusion

David came to: our only hope is in the Lord! As the old hymn reminds us: "My hope is built on nothing less than Jesus' blood and righteousness; I dare not trust the sweetest frame, but wholly lean on Jesus' name."[1]

Discover the Heart of God

- After reading Psalms 36, 37, 39, and 41, what did you notice, perhaps for the first time? What questions do you have? What did you learn about the heart of God?

- What was the oracle from God concerning sin, "speaking deeply to the consciences of wicked men" (36:1)?

- In Psalm 36, how did David describe the Lord? Who was he to David? And who is he to us?

---

1   Edward Mote, "My Hope Is Built on Nothing Less," 1834, audio recording, public domain.

- What did David encourage us not to do in Psalm 37? What are all the reasons he gave throughout this psalm for following his advice?

- What was David's "life motto" as outlined in Psalm 39? How did he live, and what did he believe about life?

- What kind of person does God bless? Who are "the first ones God helps when they find themselves in any trouble" (41:1)? What does God do for them?

Explore the Heart of God

- In what way is the message of God concerning sinful humanity true that "they are still eager to sin for the fear of God is not before their eyes" (36:1)?

- How is the divine commitment of the Lord contrasted to human faithfulness and wickedness in the rest of Psalm 36? How does this contrast relate to 36:10-12?

- Instead of following after wicked ones or being envious of them, what should we do instead? Why is this far better than fretting because of those who do evil?

- In what way will the Lord "provide for you what you desire the most" as you "make God the utmost delight and pleasure of your life" (37:4)?

- What was David saying about life in Psalm 39:3-7? What does it reveal about the heart of God, especially his conclusion in verse 7?

- Why does God bless those who regard the weak, who are kind to the poor and helpless? How does this reveal the heart of God?

Experience the Heart of God

- How have you yourself witnessed the truth of Psalm 36:1, that there is no fear of God before the eyes of wicked men?

- How have you experienced the truth of 36:5–7? Share a specific experience as an example.

- What is it that you desire the most? How might it look to "make God the most delight and pleasure of your life" (37:4) in anticipation of his providing this heart's desire?

- Does patience come easy for you, or is it hard—especially when it comes to waiting for the Lord to act, keeping on moving forward, and expecting the wicked to lose everything?

- How might it look to take the life motto David shared in 39:1–4 as your own and to hope in the Lord alone? How would it deepen your experience of the heart of God?

- How does it make you feel to know all that God does for the weak and helpless? How would you like your Kind Healer to have mercy on you and heal you?

Share the Heart of God

- Who is one person in your life who needs a deeper awareness and understanding of the heart of God? How would it look to share with them the revelation-truth in Psalm 36?

- What does it mean to those you know and their experience of the heart of God that "all may drink of the anointing from the abundance of your house! All may drink their fill from the delightful springs of Eden" (36:8)?

- How might it encourage someone to know and deepen their experience of the heart of God that "one day the wicked will be destroyed, but those who trust in the Lord will live safe and sound with blessings overflowing" (37:9)?

- If David is right that "God-lovers make the best counselors" (37:30), then with whom can you share wisdom and counsel in the ways of God?

- David is right. Our only hope is in the Lord alone! The same is true for those you know who need the Lord to hear their cries for help. Spend time crying out to the Lord on their behalf, praying for hope and help.

- Are you kind to the poor and helpless? This week, how can you share the heart of God with them by showing how the Lord protects, honors, and restores them?

CONSIDER THIS

Think about the refrain from one of our hymns of faith: "On Christ, the solid rock, I stand; all other ground is sinking sand, all other ground is sinking sand."[1] May you live by these words, recognizing that apart from Christ nothing is stable, no footing is sure. May you also live by David's words, recognizing that your hope is only in the Lord!

---

1   Mote, "My Hope Is Built on Nothing Less."